WILD about

TRUCKS AND DIGGERS

By Caroline Bingham

Stats and Facts • Top makes • Top models • Top speeds

WILD about

TRUCKS AND DIGGERS

Copyright © *ticktock* Entertainment Ltd 2003
First published in Great Britain in 2003 by *ticktock* Media Ltd.
Unit 2, Orchard Business Centre, North Farm Road, Tunbridge Wells, Kent, TN2 3XF.
We would like to thank: Jamie Asher, Peter Symons at Ice Marketing and Elizabeth Wiggans.
Picture Credits: Ainscough Crane Hire: P3br, P10-11, P31tl. Alvey & Towers: P4-5c, P6-7c, P24-25.
Caterpillar: P18-19c. Construction Photo Library: P19t. Corbis: P3bl, P8-9. JCB: P2, P22-23, P32br and OFC.
John Deere: P28-29. Komatsu: P12-13, P16-17. Letourneau Inc: P14-15c. Mack Trucks: P8.
Oshkosh: P20-21, P26-27. Peterbilt: P4.
ISBN 1 86007 362 X HB
ISBN 1 86007 368 9 PB
Printed in Italy
A CIP catalogue record for this book is available from the British Library.

CONTENTS

PETERBILT 379 RoAD TRUCK

Articulated trucks are the largest road trucks in the world. They have a front **tractor unit** and one or more **trailers**. This is a Peterbilt 379. It is one of the most famous truck brands in the world.

Peterbilt are popular trucks and have always been associated with quality. In fact they are sometimes referred to as the Rolls Royce of trucks.

The massive **engine** sits in front of the driver, inside a long **hood**.

The whole hood tips forward to allow easy access to the Peterbilt's powerful engine.

STATS AND FACTS

LAUNCHED: *1986*

ORIGIN: *USA*

MAX POWER: *600 bhp*

LENGTH: *6 metres*

WIDTH: *3 metres*

HEIGHT: *3.5 metres*

MAX SPEED: *130 mph*

FUEL CAPACITY: *841 litres x 2 tanks*

MAX LOAD: *25 tonnes*

WEIGHT: *12 tonnes*

WHEELBASE: *5.94 metres*

COST: *£150,000*

DID YOU KNOW?

Many articulated trucks have a sleeping compartment at the back of the cab.

MERCEDES-BENZ ACTROS

The German motor company Mercedes-Benz make the Actros **cabover** truck. A cabover is built with the driver's **cab** positioned above the **engine**. This design is used in countries where a truck's length is restricted.

Wind can slow a truck down. The Actros has roof **spoilers** to limit its effect. This means the truck uses less fuel.

DID YOU KNOW?

Actros trucks have been used to transport everything from dairy products to racing cars.

Because Actros trucks have to travel long distances, Mercedes-Benz make sure they are very comfortable. The cabs are even **soundproofed** to keep out engine noise.

STATS AND FACTS

LAUNCHED: *1996*

ORIGIN: *Germany*

MAX POWER: *460 bhp*

LENGTH: *18 metres*

WIDTH: *2.44 metres*

HEIGHT: *3.5 metres*

MAX SPEED: *120 mph*

FUEL CAPACITY: *600-705 litres*

MAX LOAD: *29 tonnes*

WEIGHT: *15 tonnes*

WHEELBASE: *3.9 metres*

COST: *£75,000*

Actros cabover trucks link with **semi-trailers** to carry goods. Semi-trailers have no front wheels. Instead they rest on the Actros's rear **axle**.

MACK ROAD TRAIN

Have you ever heard the saying 'built like a Mack truck'? These trucks are tough. Linked up to three or more **trailers** they form mighty road trains that haul huge loads between Australian cities. The largest of all the Mack models is called the Titan.

All Mack trucks have a bulldog mascot on the **bonnet**. The colour tells you the truck's power. The most powerful Mack has a gold bulldog. All the other models have silver mascots.

The road train has a very powerful **engine**. It is also used in Australia where the weather is very hot. This means that the truck needs a huge **radiator** to help it cool down.

STATS AND FACTS

LAUNCHED: *1977*

ORIGIN: *Australia*

MAX POWER: *600 bhp*

LENGTH: *53 metres*

WIDTH: *4 metres*

HEIGHT: *3.5 metres*

MAX SPEED: *60 mph*

TURNING CIRCLE: *Up to 25 metres*

FUEL CAPACITY: *2 x 500 litre and 2 x 265 litre tanks*

MAX LOAD: *120 tonnes (Highway), 240 tonnes (XHD)*

WEIGHT: *14 tonnes*

WHEELBASE: *5.26–6.15 metres*

COST: *£90,000*

Large fuel **tanks** allow a road train to travel thousands of miles before it needs to stop and re-fuel.

LIEBHERR LTM 1500 CRANE

This Liebherr LTM 1500 is actually a crane on wheels. It can be driven from place to place. The **arm** (also called the **jib**) extends just like a telescope and can lift loads the weight of 500 cars!

Four legs called **outriggers** hold the crane in position while it lifts. With these extended, the machine is almost 10 metres wide.

DID YOU KNOW?

The largest cranes in the world can lift a whopping 800 tonnes – that's the weight of about six fully grown blue whales!

Cranes use lifting blocks to pick up weights. This lifting block weighs more than a car. The larger the size, the heavier the load it can hold.

The LTM 1500's main jib can reach up to 84 metres. An extra jib can also be added to make the total reach an amazing 175 metres.

HAULPAK 930E DUMP TRUCK

Komatsu's Haulpak 930E Dump Truck is so big that it is not allowed to travel on roads. It has to be taken apart to get it to a new site. Trucks like this work in a quarry or a mine. They are used to move enormous loads of rock, earth or coal.

DID YOU KNOW?

As the driver's seat is nearly 5 metres above ground level, this truck has a set of stairs!

Sliding parts called **pistons** are used to tip the **bucket** up. The load then slides out. The steel bucket can hold six full-size cars.

The **engine** is heavier than the weight of the loads this dump truck carries. This stops the truck tipping over as the bucket lifts.

STATS AND FACTS

LAUNCHED: *1996*

ORIGIN: *Japan*

MAX POWER: *2,700 bhp*

LENGTH: *15.24 metres*

WIDTH: *8.23 metres*

HEIGHT: *7.32 metres*

MAX SPEED: *40 mph*

TURNING CIRCLE: *29.9 metres*

FUEL CAPACITY: *4,542 litres*

MAX LOAD: *325 tonnes*

WEIGHT: *174 tonnes*

WEIGHT OF EACH TYRE: *4.7 tonnes*

COST: *£2 million*

These machines need to have huge fuel **tanks**. They guzzle nearly nine litres of fuel every mile and are often expected to keep working all day.

LETOURNEAU L-2350 WHEEL LOADER

You could park a car in the **bucket** of LeTourneau's colossal L-2350 wheel loader. It is the biggest loader on the market. Wheel loaders are used to shift mountains of earth and rocks into the back of dump trucks.

The **bucket** can reach more than 7 metres into the air. A pick-up, **hoist** and dump will take about 25 seconds.

DID YOU KNOW?

Inside the cab, the driver operates the bucket and the steering by joystick.

The L-2350 is a real monster. Each **tyre** stands nearly four metres tall and weighs nearly eight tons. They are the largest mining tyres ever made.

A wheel loader's weight is low down. This stops the machine from tipping over on sloping ground.

STATS AND FACTS

LAUNCHED: *2001*

ORIGIN: *USA*

MAX POWER: *2,300 bhp*

LENGTH (BUCKET DOWN): *19.71 metres*

BUCKET WIDTH: *6.80 metres*

HEIGHT (BUCKET RAISED): *13.33 metres*

TURNING CIRCLE: *14.7 metres*

GROUND CLEARANCE: *46 metres*

DIGGING DEPTH: *15 metres*

MAX SPEED: *10.5 mph*

FUEL CAPACITY: *3,975 litres*

BUCKET CAPACITY: *40.52 metres³*

MAX LOAD: *72 tonnes*

WEIGHT: *190 tonnes*

COST: *£2 million*

KOMATSU D575A SUPER DOZER

If a heavy object needs a push, a bulldozer is the machine to do it. Komatsu's D575A Super Dozer is the largest of them all. More than 40 of these monsters are working in mines and quarries around the world.

The Super Dozer has **tracks** to help it ride over muddy, uneven ground. They are made up of links, which join together to form a flexible band.

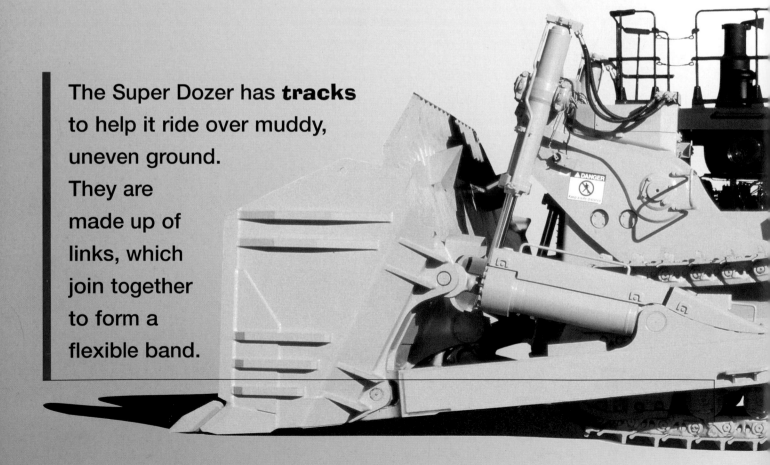

A Super Ripper attachment can tear up 2,000 tonnes of earth every hour. It has teeth that are over a metre long!

LAUNCHED: *1991*

ORIGIN: *Japan*

MAX POWER: *1,150 bhp*

LENGTH: *15 metres*

BLADE WIDTH: *7.5 metres*

BLADE HEIGHT: *3.25 metres*

NO. OF SHOES: *49 each side*

BLADE CAPACITY: *69 metres^3*

MAX SPEED: *Forward: 7.5 mph Reverse: 8.3 mph*

FUEL CAPACITY: *2,100 litres*

MAX LOAD: *28.5 tonnes*

WEIGHT: *76.54 tonnes*

COST: *£1.4 million*

The Super Dozer is more than twice as big as any other dozer on sale.

CAT 385L EXCAVATOR

Excavators are digging machines. Caterpillar produce a huge range, from mini diggers to the giant 385L shown here. A toothed **bucket** bites into the soil, scoops and tips the contents into a dump truck.

DID YOU KNOW?

The cheerful colour of these diggers dates from 1931. 'Highway yellow' made them stand out from other traffic, and was also a response to the Depression, when many people were out of work.

The excavator's **arm** has three parts. The **boom** links the machine's body to the **dipper**. At the end of the dipper is the **bucket**.

STATS AND FACTS

LAUNCHED: *1991*

ORIGIN: *USA*

MAX POWER: *428 bhp*

LENGTH: *13.08-14.30 metres*

BODY WIDTH: *4.30 metres*

CAB HEIGHT: *3.80 metres*

BUCKET CAPACITY:
2.3-4.5 metres^3

MAX DIGGING DEPTH:
6.94-10.58 metres

MAX SPEED: *4.4 mph*

FUEL CAPACITY: *990 litres*

MAX LOAD: *4 metres^3*

WEIGHT: *83.5 tonnes*

COST: *£250,000*

The 385L's **cab** is very mobile. The upper section of the 385L can turn all the way round.

The 385L turns by stopping one of the **tracks**, and continuing to move on the other track.

OSHKOSH S-SERIES MIXER TRUCK

This mighty machine is the Oshkosh S-series mixer truck. It carries six tonnes of sand, six tonnes of gravel, and 1.5 tonnes of cement. On the way to a building site, water is added. The **drum** then turns slowly to mix up concrete.

DID YOU KNOW?

The mixing system used in this machine is 2,000 years old. It was invented by a Greek scientist called Archimedes. It is called the Archimedes Screw.

This Oshkosh cement mixer sends out concrete from the front. Its **chute** can be moved in almost any direction.

STATS AND FACTS

LAUNCHED: *1999*

ORIGIN: *USA*

MAX POWER: *335 bhp*

LENGTH: *12.2 metres*

CHUTE LENGTH: *6.68 metres*

CHUTE WIDTH: *4 metres*

CHUTE HEIGHT: *4.27 metres*

MAX SPEED: *50 mph*

WATER CAPACITY: *568 litres*

FUEL CAPACITY: *190 litres*

MAX LOAD: *10.05 metres^3*

WEIGHT: *55 tonnes*

COST: *£200,000*

After the load is emptied, the inside of the drum is flushed out with water. Any cement left inside would set rock hard and ruin this expensive machine.

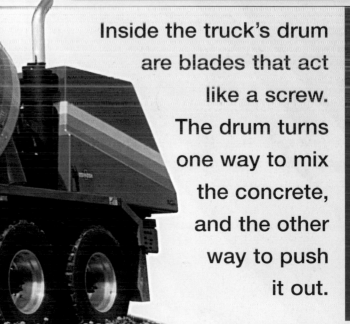

Inside the truck's drum are blades that act like a screw. The drum turns one way to mix the concrete, and the other way to push it out.

JCB BACKHOE LOADER

A backhoe loader digs trenches with its **bucket**. It then picks up the earth with its **shovel** and moves it out of the way. This machine is useful for all sorts of jobs, and is used all over the world.

DID YOU KNOW?

Look closely at a backhoe loader. It is really just a tractor with attachments at the front and back.

JCB buyers can customise their machines. They can choose the size of the **bucket** and the length of the **arm**.

JCB have a British display team called the Dancing Diggers. Five giant JCBs and two mini **excavators** perform stunts in a 30-minute show.

STATS AND FACTS

LAUNCHED: *1962*

ORIGIN: *British*

MAX POWER: *100 bhp*

LENGTH: *5.62 metres*

WIDTH: *2.36 metres*

HEIGHT: *3.61 metres*

SHOVEL WIDTH: *2.35 metres*

MAX BACKHOE DIG DEPTH: *4.67 metres*

MAX BUCKET DIG DEPTH: *0.14 metres*

MAX SPEED: *67 mph*

FUEL CAPACITY: *160 litres*

MAX LOAD: *1.1 metres^3*

WEIGHT: *7.5 tonnes*

COST: *£150,000*

The backhoe loader operator can swing the machine's arm around to work at the side of the machine.

MERCEDES RECOVERY TRUCK

If a truck breaks down or has an accident, a heavy recovery truck will take it to the garage for repairs. These gigantic trucks can haul two or three times their own weight.

Floodlights are fitted on most recovery trucks. This is because these trucks often have to rescue vehicles at night.

STATS AND FACTS

LAUNCHED: *1985*

ORIGIN: *Germany*

MAX POWER: *600 bhp*

LENGTH: *12 metres*

WIDTH: *2.44 metres*

HEIGHT: *5 metres*

MAX SPEED: *60 mph*

FUEL CAPACITY: *500 litres*

MAX LOAD: *100 tonnes*

WEIGHT: *20 tonnes*

COST: *£100,000*

Rescue trucks are built to a buyers requirements. This one was used to rescue tanks. The buyer asked for it to be fitted with a huge **engine**, and for it to be made from very strong materials.

When the recovery truck arrives at the scene, a strong metal shelf slides underneath the vehicle to be towed. It connects to the vehicle's front wheels and winches it up onto its body.

OSHKOSH SNOW BLOWER

A snow blizzard can cover a road's surface in minutes. This Oshkosh snow **blower** helps to keep a road open to traffic by breaking snowdrifts into loose powder and blowing this powder off the road.

The HB-Series is the ultimate snow mover. It has the power to shift up to 5,000 tonnes of snow every hour.

This machine has two **engines**. One drives the machine through snow drifts. The other operates the blower, which shoots snow out of the road.

STATS AND FACTS

LAUNCHED: *1991*

ORIGIN: *USA*

DRIVE ENGINE POWER: *505 bhp*

BLOWER ENGINE POWER: *650 bhp*

LENGTH: *8.52 metres*

WIDTH: *1.52 metres*

HEIGHT: *3.5 metres*

MAX SPEED: *45 mph*

FUEL CAPACITY: *2 x 473 litres*

WEIGHT: *20.4 tonnes*

WHEELBASE: *3.6/4.2 metres*

COST: *£137,000*

Unlike a car, a truck has vertical **exhaust** pipes. They are protected from damage by a heat shield.

JOHN DEERE 9750 CUMBINE

In the 1800s, harvesting a small field would take ten workers a whole day. More workers then had to collect the crop and **thresh** it to remove the grain. Today, a combine harvester will do the same job in an hour.

The grain is stored in a large **tank**, or bin, behind the **cab**. The cut stalks (the straw) are left in neat rows behind the combine, to be collected later.

DID YOU KNOW?

When the tank is full, it can be emptied into the trailer of a waiting truck in a couple of minutes.

John Deere trained as a blacksmith, but in the 1830s he designed and built a highly successful steel **plough**. The company now produce a huge range of equipment, from farm machinery to giant bulldozers.

LAUNCHED: *1999*

ORIGIN: *USA*

MAX POWER: *325 bhp*

LENGTH: *10 metres*

WIDTH: *6 metres*

HEIGHT: *5 metres*

MAX SPEED: *20 mph*

FUEL CAPACITY: *795 litres*

MAX LOAD: *10,572 litres of grain*

WEIGHT: *20.4 tonnes*

COST: *£150,000*

The harvester cuts, collects, threshes, and **winnows**. The cutting blades are on a reel six metres wide.

GLOSSARY

ARM *See boom.*

ARTICULATED TRUCK A truck that is made of two parts. It has a front tractor unit and a rear semi-trailer.

AXLE The metal rod that joins a set of wheels.

BHP Brake horse power, the measure of an engine's power output.

BLOWER A machine for producing an artificial blast or current of air by pressure.

BONNET *See hood.*

BOOM The back part of an excavator's arm, or a crane's long, extending arm.

BUCKET Scoop of an excavating machine.

CAB The part of a truck or digger that houses the driver and controls.

CABOVER A tractor unit in which the driver sits above the engine.

CHUTE A channel used to carry things downwards.

CONVENTIONAL A tractor unit in which the engine is situated in front of the driver.

DIPPER The part of an excavator's arm between the boom and the bucket.

DRUM A metal container shaped like a barrel.

ENGINE The part of a vehicle where fuel is burned to create energy.

EXCAVATOR A machine that is used to dig large holes and trenches.

EXHAUST The pipe which carries waste gases away from an engine.

FLOODLIGHTS Powerful lights that are used to light up an area at night.

HOIST Part of a machine used for lifting.

HOOD The hinged metal covering over the engine.

JIB A crane's metal arm.

JOYSTICK A hand-operated lever used to control a machine.

OUTRIGGERS Feet used to steady a truck.

PAYLOAD The load a machine is paid to carry.

PLOUGH Machine used for turning soil to prepare it for bearing crops.

PISTON A metal tube that slides in and out of a larger metal tube.

RADIATOR A device through which water or other fluids flow to keep the engine cool.

SEMI-TRAILER A trailer with no front axle.

SHOES Metal plates that are attached to each link of a crawler machine's tracks.

SHOVEL A scoop used to lift and throw loose material.

SOUNDPROOFING A means of stopping noise from getting in to a cab.

SPOILER A raised panel that limits the wind's ability to slow a truck down.

TANK A large container used to store fuel or harvested crops.

THRESH The method of separating grain from its stalk.

TRACKS Two flexible metal loops attached to some vehicles in place of wheels. They help a vehicle to grip on muddy, uneven ground.

TRACTOR UNIT Name for a tractor's cab, engine and front wheels.

TRAILER A wheeled container pulled by a truck or tractor.

TREAD The grooves and ridges in a tyre that help it to grip the road's surface.

TYRE A rubber wheel covering filled with compressed air.

WHEELBASE The distance between a tractor unit's front and rear axles.

WINCH A machine fitted with a heavy rope or chain to lift heavy objects.

WINNOW The process of separating grain from chaff (straw dust).

INDEX